Make Something UGLY ...for a change!

The definitive guide to papier/cloth mâché

DAN REEDER

with photographs by
Julie, Dan, and Jeff Reeder

GIBBS·SMITH
PUBLISHER

SALT LAKE CITY

First Edition

03 02 01 00 99   5 4 3 2 1

Text and photos copyright © 1999 Dan Reeder

Published by
Gibbs Smith, Publisher
P.O. Box 667
Layton, Utah 84041

Orders: (1-800) 748-5439
Web site: *www.gibbs-smith.com*

Edited by
Suzanne Taylor

Book design and production by
Julie E. Gassaway of 1>10 Creative House
Web site: *www.onegreaterthanten.com*

Printed and bound in China

Library of Congress Cataloguing-in-Publication Data
Reeder, Dan, 1950–
        Make something ugly—for a change: the definitive guide to papier/cloth mâché/Dan Reeder.
    p.   cm.
Summary: An illustrated, step-by-step explanation of how to
construct various ugly creations from papier and cloth mâché.
ISBN 0-87905-907-9
    1.   Papier-mâché. [1. Papier-mâché. 2. Handicraft.] I. Title.
TT871.R43   1999
745.54'2—dc21   99–17217
                                       CIP

CONTENTS

INTRODUCTION

EVERY SO OFTEN I see a "Starving Artists" sale promoted on television. The ad touts, "hundreds of gallery-quality paintings for forty bucks or less! A bonanza of beautiful seascapes, gardens, and bowls of fruit." (And the frames are nice, too.)

So why are the creators of such beauty starving? Because they sold their work for peanuts during a period of intense depression or drunkenness to multinational corporations who used sophisticated machines to reproduce the work? Or are the artists really trained monkeys who work sixteen-hour days slopping surplus lead-based paint on cheap canvas?

These are the most obvious reasons, but consider this. Maybe, just maybe, there's too much beauty in the art world today. Just too many subtle colors and pleasing patterns to take in. Too many sweet countenances and pretty faces, the *Mona Lisa* notwithstanding.

Worse yet, much of the truly beautiful artwork is saved! Year after year, decade upon decade, the stuff piles up. And we all know where that leads. Taxpayers get asked to fund new museums. Trucks haul the art around, spewing exhaust and destroying the ozone. Husbands get dragged around to "openings" to "get some culture."

At first ponder, this aesthetically pleasing problem just seems too big, too pervasive, too overwhelming for one individual to tackle. Stemming this tide of beauty seems hopeless. So what can measly little *you* do about it? You got it—MAKE SOMETHING UGLY for a change!

Such a simple idea. Such a simple way to save the planet.

But where to start? Surely it takes skill and years of training to create great ugly pieces of art, right? I mean, not all of us can look at a can of Campbell's soup and draw it really big like Andy. Or paint a single horizontal line on twenty-nine consecutive canvases like Yoko. Pretty intimidating!

Let me tell you a little secret. Hideous doesn't happen right off the bat. Sometimes it's a long painful trek from beautiful, to pretty, to cute, then, finally, to ugly—unless you're lucky enough to find a shortcut, a medium that lends itself naturally to unbecoming, and an expert ugly artist to show you the ropes.

Well, lucky you. You found this book. You must have done something nice in your previous lifetime. The techniques that will get to ugly in the shortest amount of time lie within these pages.

It begins with papier-mâché . . . well, sort of. Perhaps a brief history is in order.

HISTORICALLY SPEAKING

The French coined the phrase "papier-mâché" (pronounced *poopeye maaayshaaay*), which meant, of course, mashed paper, without the gravy. The technique involved chewing paper into slimy little wads and squishing it together into "art."

Either before or after the French, the Germans made furniture using a variation of the papier-mâché theme. This period lasted for quite a while, until one day someone said, "Das ist wirklish dumm, lass uns holz verwenden!" (*see* glossary)

Somewhere in America, a third-grade teacher made her students dip strips of newspaper into a flour-and-water soup and smear them onto balloons. For no apparent reason, this method also became known as "papier-mâché," and, for what seemed like generations, children in the United States made space helmets, birds, piggy banks, and big round things that looked like balloons covered in paper. This practice was finally outlawed to save space in the landfills for disposable diapers.

In 1984—with the publication of the prequel to this book, *The Simple Screamer: A Guide to the Art of Papier and Cloth Mâché*—a chic, contemporary, non-stupid mâché technique was born. This book outlined the *correct* use of cheap white flour and water paste with newspaper, and introduced "cloth mâché," a cloth and glue skin that revolutionized the world of mâché (well, not really)! It detailed the making of an ugly little beast, a Screamer, which has since become the standard for ugly art. Perhaps millions (vastly exaggerated) of ordinary people and royalty alike have become ugly artists. Neato!

SO UGH

With this excellent background, it's time to take your first liberating steps toward ugly art self-sufficiency. The first chapter of this book reiterates the basic steps of making a Screamer. For those of you who already own *The Simple Screamer*, you'll notice a few changes, the most obvious being that the beast being constructed is smaller. If you have a problem with this, feel free to complain to somebody. However, I have added a section called "Advanced Ugly Techniques" to make you feel like you learned something new. And the gallery in the back of the book should offer you countless new ideas for making more projects.

For all you beginners, hang on to your pants and get ready for some fun! Think ugly and get started!

P. S. So as not to disappoint those of you who thought this book was about the traditional French mâché method, because of the funny symbols above the vowels and the "i" in papier, I've included a brief how-to chapter on those antiquated papier-mâché methods. And for you Americans who figured this book would remind you how to make the cool (except for the smell) space helmet you made in the third grade, I've added some reminders of what you did as a kid as well. Sorry, I don't know how to make a papier-mâché chair.

PART ONE: *Making the Basic, Ugly, Little Screamer*

NOT UNLIKE DNA, this little beast can be viewed as the basic building block of all ugly life. The Screamer illustrated is being made with a food theme in mind. It must fit into a small silver bowl or a skillet. Your Screamer can be even smaller or much larger. The addition of the cloth-mâché skin will make your project quite strong. A preconceived theme or idea is fine, but don't feel that you must have one to begin. When the beast is finished, many times it seems to demand a certain context or prop. You'll see. So try not to think too much about the finished product as you work through each stage. Let the Screamer surprise you as it develops. Trust that the unexpected lumps and bumps will give your beast a unique personality.

It's easier to follow the process if you look at the sequence of pictures first to get an idea of where you're headed. Then proceed step by step. (Note: This smaller text is generally editorial comment and is not necessary for the building of your Screamer. But it does make the book thicker for those of you who think reading and doing are the same thing. Feel free to ignore it, especially if you're easily offended.)

PAPIER-MÂCHÉ

Step 1
Gather Materials
1. Newspaper
2. Masking tape
3. Wire clothes hangers and wire cutters
4. Cheap white flour
5. Mixing bowl
6. Water

Step 2
Crumple one sheet of paper into a ball.

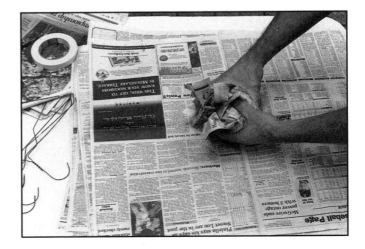

Step 3

Continue to crumple *one* sheet of paper over the other until you have the size of a "body." (Ugly Tip: Some dolls have great glass eyes. If you have young children, or know someone who does, discreetly pull out the glass eyes from a doll that the kids haven't played with for a while. Replace them with two eyes made out of clay and hope nobody notices. Put them on the table until you need them for your project. Pretend you're crazy and you think they're looking at you while you work.)

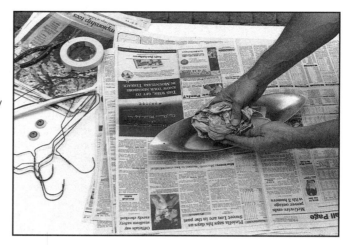

Step 4

Wrap with tape until the loose edges are held down.

Step 5

Make a head the same way, only smaller. (duh!)

Step 6
Bend part of a clothes hanger into a figure eight.

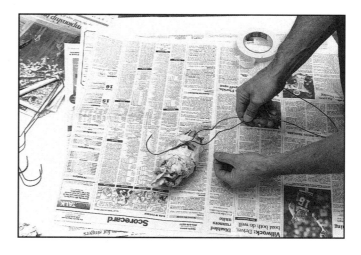

Step 7
Crumple two smaller elongated balls and stuff them into each half of the eight. Wrap with tape. This will be an arm or a leg. The clothes hanger will give it strength and allow you to bend it later at the knee/elbow without breaking.

Step 8
Make arms, legs, and a tail if you wish. Make a couple of extra balls to cut up for detail work. A tail is constructed the same way, except that the wire is pulled to a point instead of an eight. You're now ready to mâché.

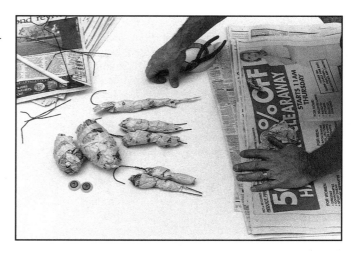

Step 9
Tear the newspaper into *wide* strips.

Step 10
Pour some cheap, white, pulverized, nutrient-neutral flour into the mixing bowl. Add water and mix to the consistency of clam chowder. (Feel how gooey the paste is! Put warm water in it! Think about how it would feel to skinny dip in a giant vat of it! Find someone who bought a bunch of Microsoft stock in 1975 and ask him if he'll fill his pool with warm paste for you! He doesn't need that pool anyway. He can use the one by the guest house at the vacation hideaway in Florida.)

Please pay attention here! This is the most important instruction in the book! Do not put the strips of paper into the paste, **ever**! You put your **hands** into the paste. Just your **hands**. See the bold print?! That's why it was invented, to **keep your paper out of the paste**! This is why your space helmet stunk in the third grade, and why your piggy bank just collapsed into itself. Your third-grade teacher probably told you to put the strips in the paste, didn't she?! Or, she told you *not* to put them in the paste, but **you weren't listening** and you did it anyway! (Did you know that she talked about you in the faculty room, about how you were a nice kid but that you just never listened?) So, globs of paste got on your strips, which created air pockets between the layers of paper and undermined the strength of your project, and the globs of flour paste rotted and smelled like your dad's feet, remember? Got it? Here's a test: **Q:** What goes in the paste? **(a) hands** (b) paper.

Step 11

Keeping your **hands** *very* wet, moisten the area you are about to mâché.

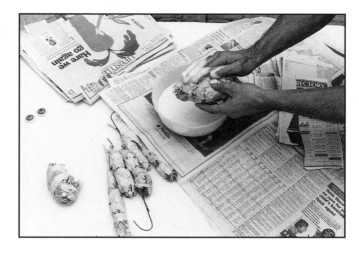

Step 12

Put on strips of paper, smoothing and soaking them with your hands as you go. Put on a new strip only after the previous one is completely wet. This will ensure that your piece dries evenly, without air pockets, and that it will be strong when dry.

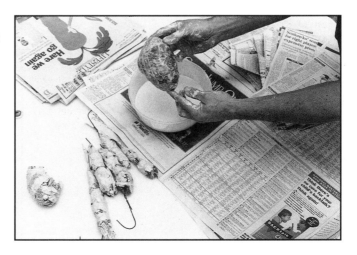

Step 13

Continue working around the ball until you have built up two or three layers of paper.

Step 14

Repeat this process for the other crumpled balls and arms, legs, and tail.

Step 15

If you do have a tail, this is a good time to add some bends to make it more interesting.

Step 16

Set the pieces aside to dry. Don't put them into the oven or the microwave. Don't sit and watch them dry. For once in your life be patient! Remember, good things come to those who wait.

(Of course, we all know about Bob who waited to get that new boat so he could sail to Hawaii after he retired, but then got run over by a truck on the way to buy it. That doesn't mean it will happen to you ... I don't think.)

ARMS AND LEGS

Step 1
Materials for the arms/legs
1. A few more wire hangers and the wire cutters.
2. Your dried body parts.
3. Masking tape.
4. Small serrated knife. A steak knife is ideal for this purpose. It doesn't have to be sharp, the serration saws the mâché balls.
5. Some newspapers or an old phone book.
(The doll eyes are still looking at you. Cover one of the eyes with your thumb . . . it looks like it's winking at you. You understand. You look pretty cute today.)

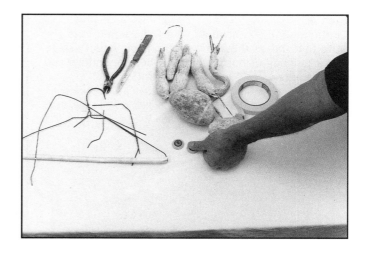

Step 2
Cut hangers into sections for fingers and toes. Make them long enough to have a bit of extra wire sticking out at the end.

Step 3
Twist a piece of paper around the wire and wrap with tape.

Step 4

Continue until you have all your fingers and toes. Note that this is the same method you would use to make tongues or horns, or any other appendage you might want to bend into shape later.

(Did you ever notice that cartoon characters have only four fingers on each hand? Sometimes four looks more like five than five. Truth really is stranger than fiction.)

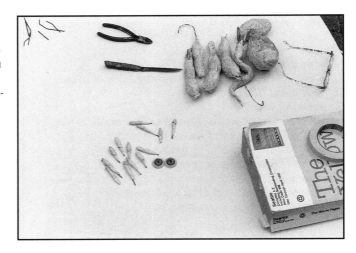

Step 5

Crumple a small sheet of paper and flatten it slightly for the main part of a hand or foot.

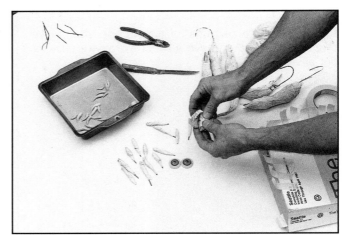

Step 6

Secure each finger or toe to the ball by putting a strip of tape on either side in crisscross fashion.

Step 7

Continue adding the fingers. Place the thumb a little lower on the hand than the rest of the fingers.

Step 8

Match a hand with an arm and wrap tape around the wrist until the two are connected.

Step 9

Put together all of your arms and legs in this fashion.

HEADS

Step 1

Materials for your basic ugly little head

1. Teeth. There are many types of materials on the market you can use for teeth, from oven-baked clay to plasticene products. They can be found at any hobby/craft store.

2. The mâché ball you made for the head.

3. The "table's" eyeballs. Doll or stuffed-animal eyes work great, but anything round will work, like drawer knobs, marbles, or beads. The easiest way to get eyes is to make them out of the same material you used for the teeth.

4. The serrated knife.

5. Masking tape.

Step 2

Make your teeth by rolling small pieces of clay between your fingers. Make a small point at the end, or imprint a crease if you want a molar.

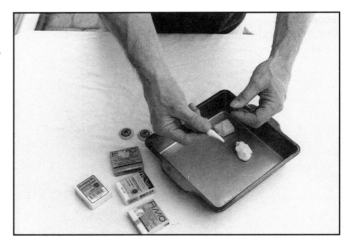

Step 3

For eyes, just roll into a sphere.

Step 4
Use these to replace the ones you stole.

Step 5
Make a crooked cut all around the head ball.

Step 6
Pull the halves apart and yank out the wad of paper inside. These half shells will be the jaws of your Screamer.

Step 7
Secure the teeth around the jaw by wrapping a piece of tape on either side in crisscross fashion.

Step 8
Repeat until both halves are complete.
(Make your mouth tell the table's eyes to "Quit watching, dammit!")

JUST A HEAD

Stop right here for a minute. Time to take stock of your life. I know, you've always set big goals for yourself. You started out thinking you'd be president of the United States. Then it was president of a large company. Then it was manager at the local supermarket. Then you just wanted a job, any job. Let me save you the price of your next self-help book. You don't need to be the president to be happy! You don't even need to boss the working class around to feel important. And you don't need to finish an entire little beast to make a great piece of ugly art! If you're feeling stressed about where you're going to find the time to make *all* those fingers and arms and stuff, just relax. Make just a head and move on with your life. After all, is there anything more desirable than, say, a head in a jar?

Now if you're actually going to follow my advice and just make a head (you wimp) at least make a really nice one. This section is inserted to help you make a perfect, stand-alone, ugly little human head. (Your head *could* stand alone if you made little feet for it!) Later on, if you actually do become president, have one of your aides make a body for you.

Step 1
For a truly amazing look, use real teeth or facsimiles of real teeth, dentures, bridges, or baby teeth. Ask around, see what pops up (or out). Cows, sharks, dead pets all have nice teeth.

Step 2
Cut a papier-mâché ball in half and tape the teeth into the shell. If you do find some used dentures, you'll want to ugly them up. Breaking out a few teeth helps a lot.

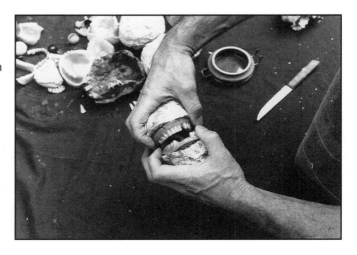

Step 3

Tape on the eyes. Shown is one porcelain drawer knob and one marble. Different-size eyes are very unbecoming.

(Be on the lookout for more elaborate eyes. As already mentioned, some dolls and stuffed-animal eyes can be spectacular. Mannequin or taxidermist eyes can also be used with terrific results. If you're really, really lucky, the guy who gave you his dentures also has a glass eye you can use!)

Step 4

Slice off pieces of one of the extra mâché balls.

Step 5

Tape them on for ears, noses, cheeks, and chins.

Step 6
When putting the cloth into the ears and nostrils, poke holes into the mâché ball so that you can shove oversized pieces of cloth into them. This will create creases and wrinkles.

Step 7
Fold pieces of the cloth and lay them over and under the eyes to create eyelids.

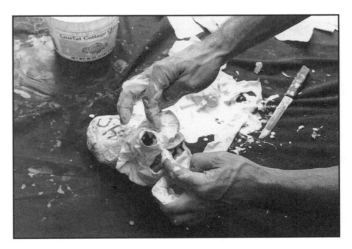

Step 8
Fill the uncovered spots with small pieces of cloth.
Put the head in a warm place to dry.
Paint as explained in the painting section.

Step 9

You can get a variety of old wigs and hairpieces at any thrift store. Take your little head to the store with you to try them out. Try something blond and stinky.

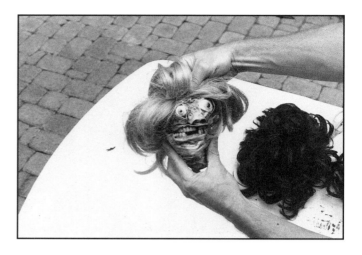

Step 10

Maybe brunette.

Step 11

How about a few feathers? Don't be silly.

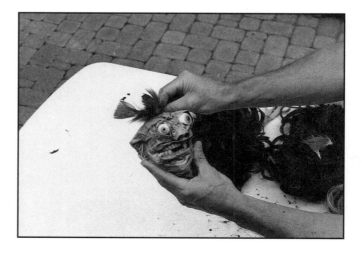

Step 12
Settle on a hairstyle that looks like your own. Use hot glue or white glue to hold it on.

Step 13
Realize that you're out of date by about twenty years, then reluctantly cut your hair.

Step 14
Pretend you're a famous trendsetting hairstylist in New York City!

Step 15

Pretend you expertly trim your client's nose hairs without him knowing, as the self-absorbed little jerk blithers on and on about how great he is.

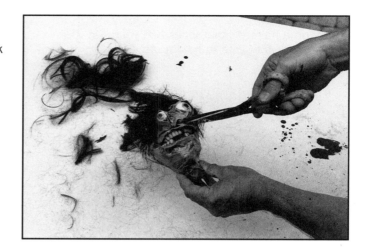

Step 16

"You sure do nice work!" he says as he leaves. He gives you a big tip! Now you think he's a good-lookin' nice guy!

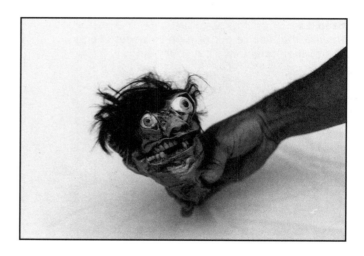

25

ASSEMBLY

If you're still on track to make the whole beast, gather all your body parts. You're going to be amazed by the time you reach the end of this section.

Step 1
Cut a large hole in the body ball and punch in the newspaper to create a cavity.

Step 2
Insert the back of the jaw into the hole . . .

Step 3
. . . and stretch pieces of tape underneath and onto the body.

Step 4
Put the other half of the head on top of the jaw and tape.

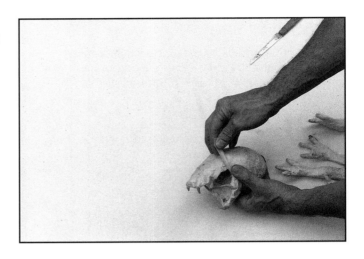

Step 5
Similarly, cut a hole in the body that is slightly smaller than the diameter of a thigh.

Step 6
Cut off the excess wire on the leg.

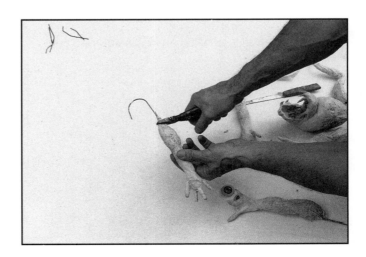

Step 7

Push the leg into the hole.

Step 8

Stretch tape between the leg and the body. Don't skimp on the tape here. Make sure the pieces of tape overlap and go in different directions for strength.

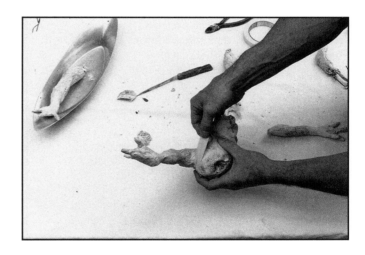

Step 9

Do the same with the other leg.

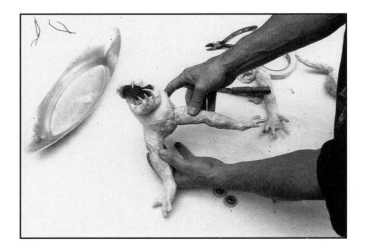

Step 10
Then each arm.

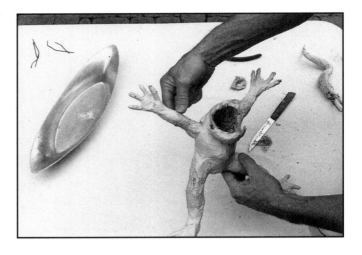

Step 11
Bend the arms and legs into different positions until you get an "attitude" that you like.

Step 12
Tape little balls of squished paper where the knees or elbows break. Accentuate these to make kneecaps and knobby elbows.

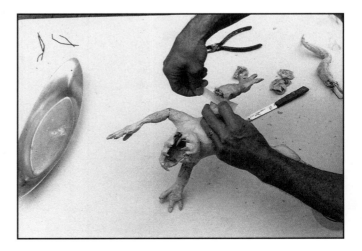

Step 13
Tear the eyeballs away from the table and tape them onto the face of your beast.

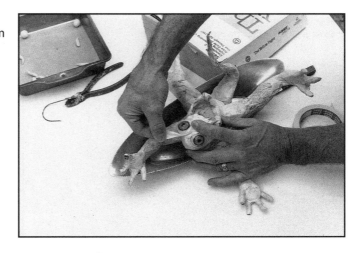

Step 14
Tape on a nose. This can be a small crumpled piece of paper, or an extra tooth, eyeballs, or anything else lying around the house.

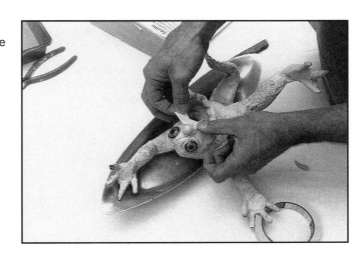

Step 15
A bent piece of cardboard makes a great ear.

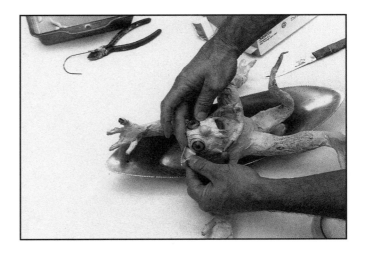

Step 16
Extra teeth make perfect horns.

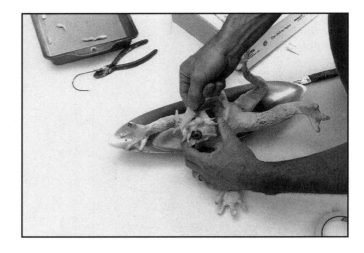

Step 17
If you're using a bowl, a skillet, or some other prop, adjust him so that he fits comfortably.
(Remember, he must spend his eternity in that wretched thing, frozen in time, with nobody who really cares whether he's dirty or happy, or fulfilled . . . sort of like the rest of us.)

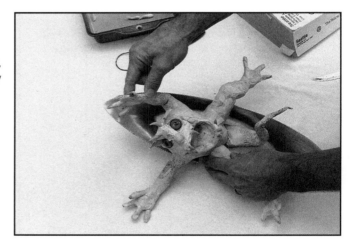

CLOTH MÂCHÉ

No matter how much paint or lacquer is used on a traditional papier-mâché piece of art, it will be inflexible, brittle, and easily breakable. Adding a skin of cloth dipped in glue not only fixes that problem but allows for much more detail. It will make your project strong while keeping it somewhat flexible and resilient to abuse. It can be easily fashioned into wrinkles and bulges, which are the staples of ugly art.

The best and cheapest cloth to use is an old bedsheet. You can find old sheets in thrift stores, two aisles past the wool, grunge-rocker hat section. Look for the most-worn sheets, the kind you can tear with your fingers. Ignore the stains.

Step 1
Material list for cloth mâché
1. A quart of all-purpose white glue. A cheap generic brand is best.
2. An old bedsheet torn into strips and rectangles of various sizes.
3. Scissors.
4. A container for the glue.
5. Your little Screamer.

Step 2
Unlike in the papier-mâché process, the cloth strips **are** put into the glue. Soak the pieces of cloth completely and squeeze out the excess.

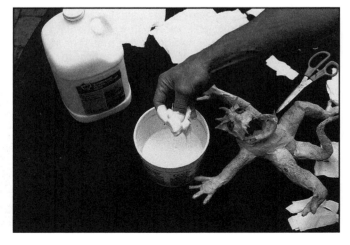

Step 3
Put a small strip of cloth around each tooth.

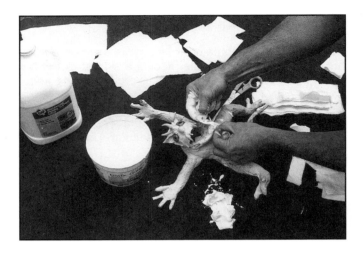

Step 4
Soak a piece of cloth that is larger than the mouth.

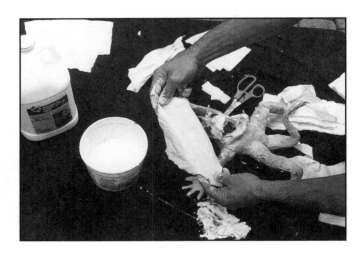

Step 5
Stuff it into the little guy's mouth. The cloth will wrinkle up and make the inside of the mouth interesting. Press the edges of the wet cloth up against the base of the teeth.

Just a Head GALLERY

Centerpiece for Mom

Mom's Head (Dad's still working on the body.)

Good Heads Under Her Shoulders

Head for the Diamond Lane

Life on a Silver Platter

Get Your Heads Straight

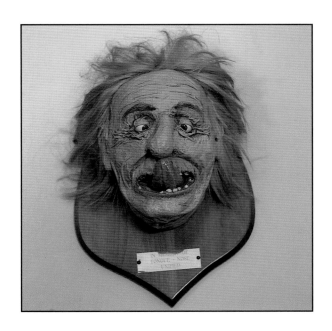

Relativitively Speaking

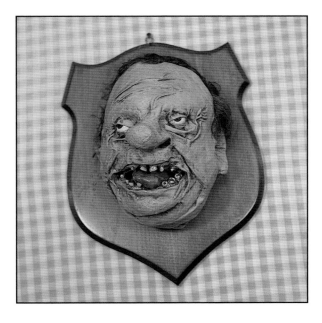

Mount Seymore

Ugly Art GALLERY

Polly Got a Squawker

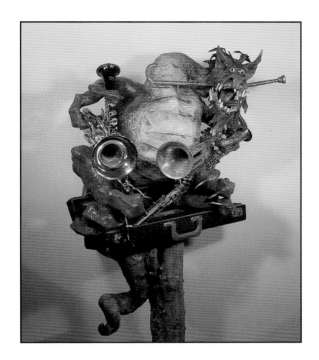

Horns of a Dilemma

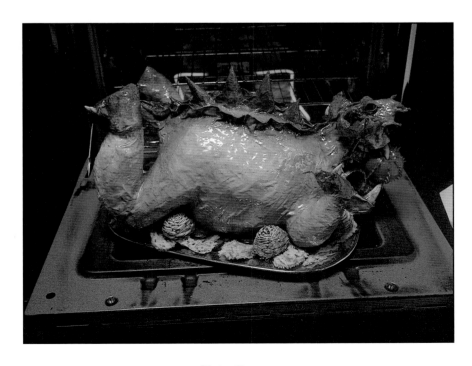

Main Corpse

Rubbed the Wrong Way

Organized

George and the Dragon

Bobby and the Dragon

Doctor Barbie and the Dragon

Baby Ducky and the Sea Dragon

Baby's Baby and the Red Dragon

Little Willy and the Dragon Queen

Little William and the Drag Queen

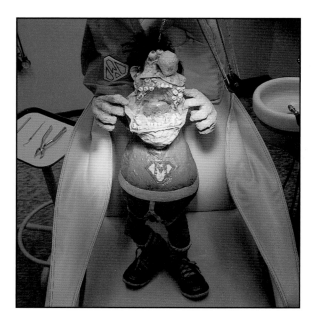

Molar Man

Ned and Ted

Kooky Jar

ICU2

Family Tree

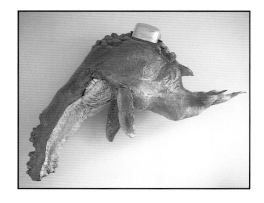

Pacific Toasterback

Fish & Chips

Fudgestuckle

See You Sundae

Cheep Date

Piggy Bankasis

Brace Yourself

Desserted

Eggsontoastwithcoffeeoverit

Duh-Duh Bird

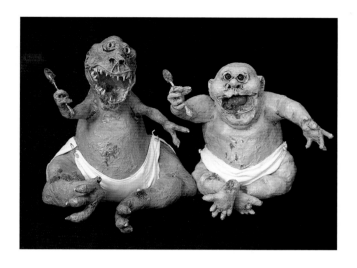

Dueling Babies

Tyrannosaurus Eatalotacus

Historical Mâché
GALLERY

Papier-Mâché

Helmet

Piggy

Birdy

Step 6

As a rule, fantastic wrinkles can be created anytime a piece of cloth is applied that is too large for the surface it is covering. Of course, the more wrinkles the better. Bags under the eyes automatically appear as you drape rectangular strips under round eyes.

Step 7

Wrap thin strips of cloth around and in between each finger and toe.

Step 8

Using the various-sized strips and rectangular pieces of cloth, work your way down the arms . . .

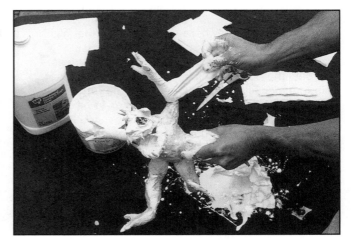

Step 9

. . . then up the legs.

Step 10

Cover the body and all remaining areas that need skin.

Step 11

Put the project somewhere warm to dry. This might take a couple of days. Note that this cloth skin could be applied in stages. Do the arms and legs one day, the body the next, and the face after that. This is especially helpful if you want the arms and legs and various parts of the Screamer to be solid and strong as you work on other places. You'll be amazed how light and durable your beast will be when the glue is completely dry.

PAINTING

Step 1
Painting Materials
1. Paint. Any paint will do, but latex is best with the cloth-and-glue combination.
2. Brushes. A large one for the body and a small one for detail.

Step 2
Pick a color for the mouth and splash some paint into it.
(Do this like you're in a race, fast and furious. Don't worry if the paint gets all over the place. Right now, the only thing that matters is getting the beast finished.)

Step 3
Imagine light shining over your beast. Using a very wet brush, paint the undersides, the places where the shadow would be, under the arms and chin, inside the hands, the back of the legs, etc.

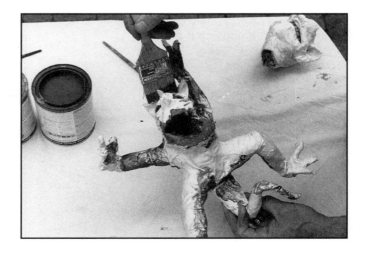

Step 4
Use a deep shade of pink for a little humanlike head.

Step 5
While the paint is still wet, dip your brush into the lighter paint.

Step 6
Slosh it onto the unpainted areas.

Step 7

Add some white to the pink mix and highlight the tops of the wrinkles and bags under the eyes.

Step 8

Blend the colors where they meet. Be careful, however, not to overwork the blending or your project will become just a monotone mess.

Step 9

When the Screamer is dry, paint the teeth white (and the eyeballs if you're not using glass ones). Let the white paint dry. If you used dentures, scrape the paint off with the tip of a knife to retain the natural appearance of the teeth.

Step 10
For a truly dramatic effect, "blackwash" the project. Mix a small amount of water with black paint. Paint part of your Screamer with the mixture.

Step 11
Wipe the black mixture off the high spots with a damp rag before it dries.

Step 12
There's nothing like a little dirt to bring out the natural color in your face.

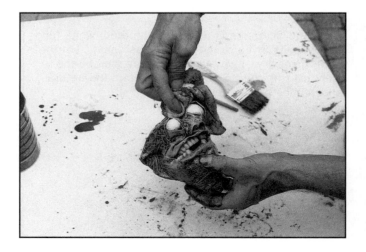

Step 13

If you used glass eyes, use the end of a knife or sharp instrument to scrape off the paint. Latex paint will peal off and your Screamer will come alive.

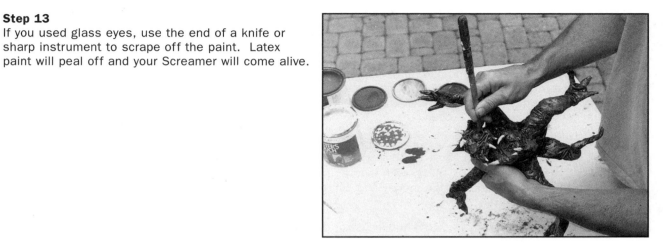

Step 14

If you painted the eyes white, add irises and pupils.

PART TWO: *Ugly Food for Thought*

IF YOU THINK about it, food and Screamers have a great deal in common. Have you ever *really* looked at what people put into their mouths? Egad! Let's face it, most food doesn't look very appetizing. Imagine you came from a different planet and were viewing Earth-food for the first time. Uttbugly! (If you actually *are* from another planet, you know what I mean.)

Still having trouble with this? How about oysters! Q.E.D.

The point is, presentation is everything—with food and ugly art. Screamers and food scenarios go perfectly together, sorta like bricks and mortar, money and rich people, "fat free" and lying.

Two examples follow:

DESSERTED

Step 1
Find your Screamer a lovely, pewterlike, dessert bowl.

Step 2
Make a couple of papier-mâché balls to use for ice cream. Paint them vanilla and chocolate.
(For those of you who flunked dessert art in high school, vanilla is white with a teeny bit of yellow, chocolate is brown, which is red, blue, and yellow, or all the colors mixed together, whichever you prefer. Recall that vanilla and chocolate are on opposite sides of the color wheel.)

Step 3

Squish one of the ice-cream balls so that it fits over the belly of the little beast. Put a bit of white glue on the bottom of the ball (or use hot glue if you can't wait) and press it on. If you have a double decker, do the same for the other ice-cream ball.

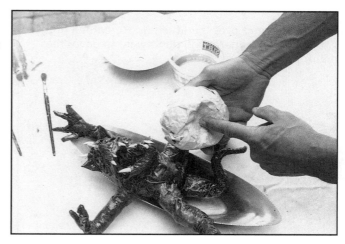

Step 4

Make some gooey chocolate syrup by mixing a rich dark brown: red, yellow, and blue, with an emphasis on the red and blue.

Step 5

Mix in some white flour to thicken the mixture.

Step 6

Spoon the syrup over the little guy. Be careful not to get carried away here. You don't want to cover the entire project.

Step 7

If you have a hard brown rubber extension cord and a utility knife, you can shave off some truly realistic-looking chocolate chunks!

WARNING!! Do not to stand in a pail of water while holding the electric cord in your mouth when it is plugged into an outlet while adjusting the knife with the blade exposed!

Step 8

Get some brilliant white silicone caulk to use for whipped cream (unless you're on a diet). Cut off the end of the tube a little farther up than for normal use.

Step 9

Using your utility knife, cut little "Vs" in the end of the tube. These will add a swirl to the caulk as it comes out.

Step 10

Squeeze out a dollop of caulk onto the belly. Add other little piles of caulk where you see fit.

Step 11
Put a plastic strawberry or cherry on top while the mixture is still wet.

Step 12
Sprinkle the fake chocolate chunks onto the wet caulk. Sweet!

ANOTHER FOOD THOUGHT: EGGS ON TOAST

Step 1
Grab an old skillet lying around the house.

Step 2
Fry two eggs, sunny-side up, in the skillet. Put the Screamer in the middle.

Step 3
Make a pot of heart-palpitatingly strong coffee. Pour yourself a cup. Add a little milk.
(Just to be contrary, stir opposite the Coriolis force for your hemisphere. Doesn't it feel good to conquer nature?)

Step 4
Make two pieces of slightly burnt toast. Butter lavishly.

Step 5
Add a layer of refined sugar.

Step 6
Slide the eggs onto the toast.

Step 7
Pour the coffee over the eggs. I'm telling you, this is delicious!

PART THREE: *Advanced Ugly Techniques*

MANY ARTISTS ARE reluctant to give away trade secrets. They are worried that if they gave away a technique like "painting up," every Tom, Dick, and Harry would be painting the ceilings of their chapels. And they're deathly afraid of exposing an artistic weakness like "I have trouble with hands," for fear nobody would buy their marble statues of beautiful but armless women.

I can tell you that ugly artists stand apart in this regard. They're not afraid to expose themselves. And they don't mind sharing their special art techniques and methods. Maybe it's because they know that once the proverbial secret art beans are spilled, everyone will realize that the "secrets" weren't worth the raggedy old paint-spattered, glue-covered pants they were spilled on! Obscure? You betcha!

To prove this point, anyway, I've detailed every major secret there is to be revealed about papier- and cloth-mâché ugly art. Still, don't tell your friends.

HEAD FITTING

Step 1
Chances are that this will happen to you at some point in your life. You make a nice little head and find the absolute perfect jar to put it in. To your complete horror, it won't fit! Does your life as an artist come to an end? Not if you follow these steps!

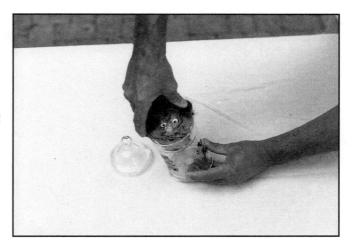

Step 2
Stick your foot by your mouth.

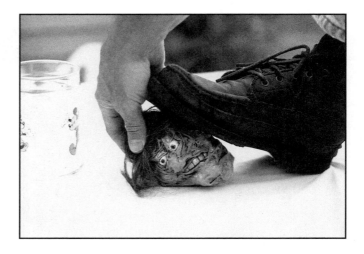

Step 3
Push down.

Step 4
Say to your little friend, "My, don't you look great! Have you lost weight?"

Step 5
Then put him in a jar for the rest of his life.

WEBBING

Frog feet, fish fins, and dragon wings need a special treatment for realism. Skip the papier-mâché here and use only the cloth dipped in glue.

Step 6
This begins much like making fingers and toes. Use clothes-hanger wire and strips of paper. Twist the paper around the piece of wire and add tape. Create a taper by adding more paper at the bottom than at the top.

Step 7
If you're making fins, stick the wires into the body of the fish and tape. If you're making webbed hands or bat/dragon wings, use the tapered pieces as long fingers.

Step 8
Dip a large rectangular piece of cloth into the white glue and drape it over the wire structure.

Step 9

Press the cloth between the wire to emphasize the cusps.

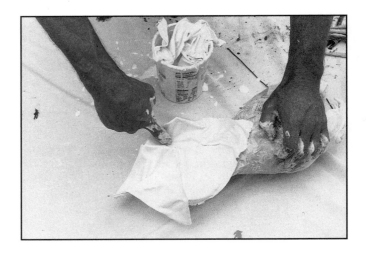

Step 10

Let this dry completely.

Step 11

Cut a serrated pattern between the spines with scissors. Add some small strips of cloth and glue to the back side of the webbing to cover the spines.

SCALES

If you really want to go the extra mile on that fish or dragon, add some scales. It will be well worth the effort. The detail will take an ugly little beast and, well, make an ugly little beast with scales! It will also add substantially more strength to your sculpture. Folding the cloth before applying it as scales is like putting on several layers at once.

Step 1
Cut cloth into small squares.

Step 2
Dip each square piece of cloth into the glue and squeeze out the excess. Fold two corners toward the middle to make a point.

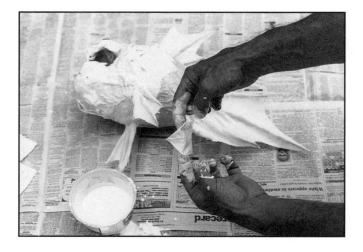

Step 3

Place the scales on the project starting at the tail end of a fish or the ankles of a dragon.

Step 4

Place rows of scales onto the body like a bricklayer places bricks—one point in between two others.

Step 5

Work your way up the body. Let it dry.

Step 6
Use the backwashing technique to accentuate the scales after the project has been painted.

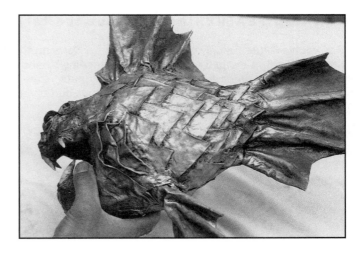

Step 7
Then add a really big tongue.

TAR AND FEATHERING (without the tar)

Say you've made an ugly bird. (This is just a Screamer with a long neck and skinny legs.) Now you want to add that final realistic touch: feathers. I'm going to show you how to do it. It isn't that hard. But you'll hate me in the end. These feathers will drive you nuts. They fly all over the house, get into your nose, your ears, any uncovered orifice. And if you eat a peanut butter and jelly sammich while you work . . . well, cluck, cluck, cluck.

So I warned you. Still, if feathering becomes the object of your life, like climbing Mt. Everest or something, then go right ahead. Just remember that there aren't any Sherpas around to do all the hard work and then let you have the glory.

Step 1
Paint the face and legs before the feathering. Then go to any hobby/craft store and pick up a few bags of feathers. Hot glue is the best way to apply them, although white glue will work.

Step 2
Start low on the leg. Put a small amount of glue on the bird and put the stem of the feather into it. Hold for a couple of seconds.

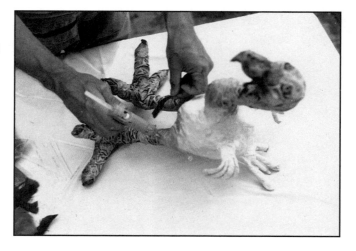

Step 3

Add another dab of glue and another feather.
(Put your glue gun down into the middle of the feather pile so that the next time you pick it up, it is just a mass of feathers.)

Step 4

Work your way up the leg overlapping the feathers like you did with the scales.

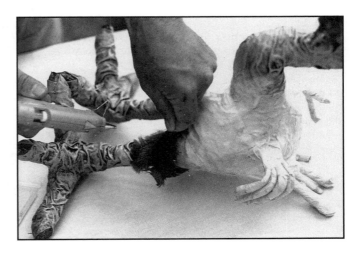

Step 5

When you get to the trunk of the bird, go to the end of the wing and begin putting on long feathers. Work back to the trunk. Then go back to the top of the legs and add feathers to the torso and up the neck. Clean up the horrendous mess, if you can.

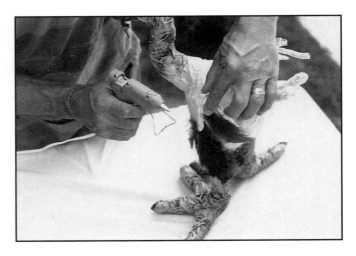

PART FOUR: *Historical Mâché Workshop*

PAPIER-MÂCHÉ

Êtes-vous prêt à faire du papier-mâché? Okeedokie. Below is a brief description of how the French did it. (This is not a claim of historical accuracy.)

Step 1
Get your kids to chew up a wad of newspaper. Tell them you'll give 'em a buck if they can chew up a pound.

(Remember, they're kids. They don't know how much a pound is! When they can't stand chewing anymore, tell them, "Sorry, that's not quite a pound." Give them the buck anyway to stop the crying. Tell them that if they don't try hard in school that's what they'll have to do for a living.)

Step 2
Squish some of the yucky chewed paper into a nice shape.

Step 3
Voilà! Display proudly.

"Art"

THIRD-GRADE MÂCHÉ

What you did in grade school went something like this.

Step 1
Tear some newspaper into thin strips.

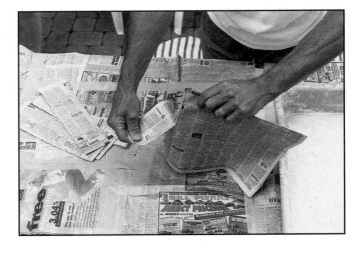

Step 2
Blow up some balloons.

Step 3
Convince the kids that this kind of mâché is really different than the French version and invite them to help. Have them stick their hands into the goo.
(Recall that kids are very trusting and have short memories.)

Step 4
Smear the flour-and-water paste onto the balloon. **Don't** put the balloon into the paste to save time.

Step 5
Give in to your six-year-old's demand and let her do it **her own way**.

Step 6
Use your best nonjudgmental tone of voice to remind your daughter that you are always right.

Step 7
Resume the project with your youngest daughter, who always follows directions. Apply strips of paper to the balloon, wetting each piece with your hands.

Step 8
Every so often, put the strips of paper into the paste to ensure that there will be big globs of paste that will never really dry inside the project.

Step 9
Continue adding way more layers than is necessary, and let the ball dry. Cut up the balls and make stuff.
(Admire the symmetry. Think about how neat it is that everyone's balloon project looks exactly the same. Wouldn't Karl Marx like this kind of art?)

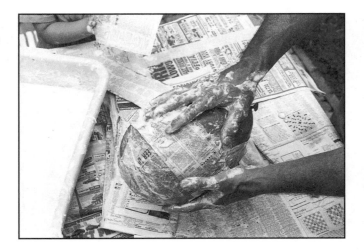

GLOSSARY

Êtes-vous prét à faire du papier-mâché? (et-vü-pra-blah-blah-blah) *sentence*: [French] "you wanna papier-mâché?"

okeedokie ('o-ke-do-ke) *syn.*: yep. *ant.*: nope.

u ('yü) *n.*: Ugly, without the gly.

Ugh ('eg) *n.*: A grunt to indicate disgust; a readiness to begin something disgusting. **ugher** *n.*

ugly (eg'-le), *adj.*: Offensive to stiff-minded people; **uglily** *tungtwstr.* <Ugly is in the eye of the beholder.> <The beholder has *ugly* eyes.> <The dog was *uglily* as sin.> <The *ugly* psychic hotline-1-900-IMA-NIT-TWIT>.

ugliquitous (eg-'lik-wət-əs) *adj.*: being ugly everywhere at the same time; constantly ugly; ugly as far as the eye can see; WIDESPREAD UGLY—**ugliquitous-ly** *adv.* —**ugliquitousness** *n.*

ukulele (yü-kə-la-le) *n.*: ugly little guitarlike thing; **ukulelar** *adv.*

uttbugly (et-'bug-le) *n.*: pig-latin insult; **uttbugliest** *adj.*

wirklish ('veer-klish) *no idea*: [German] really <*wirklish dumm*—really, really dumb>.

holz (holetzzz) *n.*: [German] wood.

verwenden (Far-voon-dən) *v.*: [German] use.

voilá ('Vü-wä-lä) *adj.*: [French] wahoo.

papier ('püp-eye-ear) *adj.*: [French] paper: [American] paper misspelled

squish (skwish) *v.*: smush

www.uglyart.com ('dubya-dubya-dubya-dät-eg-le-ärt-dät-käm) *site*: please, never!

â slith**er**   ā slau**ther**   a slather   å slthr   î slith**er**   Ÿ **slitherer**
ü **you**   ä **are**   e n**u**t   ä b**a**ll $ money

About the
AUTHOR

DAN REEDER (pictured above, in a ten-year-old, fuzzy picture chosen to make him look younger, with his beast "Tyrannosaurus Eatalotacus") is an ugly artist living in Seattle, Washington. In 1972 Dan embarked upon a quest to understand the universe. He figured he'd start where Einstein left off, working on a system of equations that would explain the relationship between the various forces at work in the cosmos. But, among other things, he needed to do the dishes first. So one thing led to another until, one beautiful moment, Dan stumbled upon the use of cloth dipped in glue as a skin for his papier-mâché sculptures. He would have yelled, "Eureka!" but he didn't know what it meant. Like Einstein, he published his pioneering work. In 1984 he wrote the book *The Simple Screamer: A Guide to the Art of Papier and Cloth Mâché*. He continues to work in the medium and has since forgotten about the Unified Field Theorems, although he did make Einstein's head using his mâché technique. When asked about it, Dan says, "Two breakthroughs in one lifetime would be pretty unlikely." He is known around the Pacific Northwest as Dan "the monster man," probably because "Dan" and "man" rhyme.